© 2024 Ijana Nathaniel

All rights reserved. No part of this vision board journal may be reproduced, distributed, or transmitted in any form or by any means, including photocopying, recording, or other electronic or mechanical methods, without the prior written permission of the author, except in the case of brief quotations embodied in critical reviews and certain other noncommercial uses permitted by copyright law.

First Edition, December 2024

Ijana Nathaniel
Bookijananathaniel@gmail.com

ISBN: 978-0-9973841-1-6

Cover design by Ijana Nathaniel Solutions
Interior layout by Ijana Nathaniel Solutions

Printed in the United States

This is a work of personal reflection and goal-setting. Names, characters, places, and incidents either are products of the author's imagination or are used fictitiously. Any resemblance to actual persons, living or dead, events, or locales is entirely coincidental.

"Dreams plus action equal success." - Ijana Nathaniel

table of CONTENTS

01 — **Introduction**
Welcome letter from the author.

02 — **About The Author**

03 — **Day 1 - 5**
Intentions, Core values, Visualizing, Beliefs, Confidence

04 — **Day 6 - 10**
Change, Gratitude, Boundaries, Passion, Resillience

05 — **Day 11 - 15**
Creativity, Self-care, Mindfulness, Relationships, Forgiveness,

06 — **Day 15 - 21**
Strength, Patience, Joy, Authenticity, Action, Reflection

HEY THERE, GOAL DIGGER!

Congratulations on picking up this journal! You're about to embark on a 21-day adventure that's all about unlocking your potential and crafting the life you've always envisioned. Think of this journal as your personal GPS—guiding you through the winding roads of self-discovery, goal-setting, and a sprinkle of magic along the way. Each page is packed with powerful affirmations, thought-provoking questions, and fun activities designed to ignite your motivation and boost your confidence. So grab your favorite pen, get comfy, and let's turn those dreams into reality—one fabulous day at a time! Ready? Let's dive in!

Ijana Nathaniel

ABOUT THE AUTHOR

Ijana Nathaniel

Ijana Nathaniel is a distinguished female leader who has significantly impacted the education sector. She is the founder and president of Dare 2 Dream Leaders Inc., a nonprofit organization established in 2010. Ijana has hosted annual youth summits and pitch contests for middle and high school students through the organization. Ijana serves as an Adjunct professor at CUNY NYC College of Technology. She is an accomplished public speaker and has been invited to speak at prestigious universities such as Penn State, Fordham University, and the University of Arkansas, as well as at the Department of Mental Health and Hygiene.

Ijana holds an undergraduate degree in Human Services from CUNY New York City College of Technology, a Masters in Organizational Leadership from Nyack College, and is currently pursuing a Doctorate of Education in Leadership & Innovation at Marymount University. Her academic qualifications are an integral part of her career, as she uses them to teach her students and youth in the nonprofit organization to be leaders. Her motto is "What would you do if you knew you could not fail."

As a college professor, Ijana is proud of the opportunity to impact her students beyond the classroom. Her positive energy, ambitious nature, kindness, and outgoing personality are some of the traits that make her stand out as a leader in her field. When she's not working, Ijana enjoys spending time with her two children, indulging in karaoke, and traveling.

DAY 01
SETTING INTENTIONS

"I AM OPEN TO THE ENDLESS POSSIBILITIES THAT LIFE OFFERS."

WHAT DO I WANT TO ACHIEVE IN THE NEXT YEAR?

Goal 1

Goal 2

Goal 3

Describe how achieving these goals will change your life.

DAY 02

IDENTIFYING CORE VALUES

> **"I ALIGN MY ACTIONS WITH MY VALUES."**

WHAT ARE MY CORE VALUES?

01

02

03

LIST FIVE VALUES THAT ARE MOST IMPORTANT TO YOU.

_____

_____

_____

_____

_____

_____

_____

_____

_____

_____

HOW DO THESE VALUES INFLUENCE YOUR DAILY DECISIONS?

DAY 03
VISUALIZING SUCCESS

"I SEE MY DREAMS CLEARLY AND VIVIDLY."

WHAT DOES SUCCESS LOOK LIKE TO ME?

CREATE A SMALL SKETCH OR WRITE A DESCRIPTION OF YOUR IDEAL LIFE.

Sketch 1   **Sketch 2**   **Sketch 3**

How can I incorporate elements of this vision into my current life?

DAY 04

OVERCOMING LIMITING BELIEFS

> **"I RELEASE ALL BELIEFS THAT NO LONGER SERVE ME."**

WHAT BELIEFS ARE HOLDING ME BACK?

_____

_____

_____

_____

_____

_____

_____

_____

_____

WRITE DOWN ONE LIMITING BELIEF AND REFRAME IT INTO A POSITIVE STATEMENT.

WHAT EVIDENCE DO I HAVE THAT CONTRADICTS THIS LIMITING BELIEF?

_____
_____
_____
_____
_____

_____
_____
_____
_____
_____

_____
_____
_____
_____
_____

DAY 05
BUILDING CONFIDENCE

> **"I TRUST IN MY ABILITIES AND STRENGTHS."**

WHEN HAVE I FELT MOST CONFIDENT?

_____

_____

_____

_____

_____

_____

_____

_____

_____

LIST THREE PAST ACHIEVEMENTS THAT MAKE YOU PROUD.

Moment 1 **Moment 2** **Moment 3**

How can I use these achievements to boost my confidence today?

DAY 06

EMBRACING CHANGE

> "I WELCOME CHANGE AS AN OPPORTUNITY FOR GROWTH."

HOW DO I TYPICALLY RESPOND TO CHANGE?

_____
_____
_____
_____
_____
_____
_____
_____
_____
_____
_____

REFLECT ON A RECENT CHANGE AND LIST THREE POSITIVE OUTCOMES IT BROUGHT.

_____
_____
_____
_____
_____
_____

_____
_____
_____
_____
_____
_____

_____
_____
_____
_____
_____
_____

DAY 07
CULTIVATING GRATITUDE

> "I AM GRATEFUL FOR ALL THAT I HAVE AND ALL THAT IS YET TO COME."

WHAT AM I GRATEFUL FOR TODAY?

WRITE DOWN FIVE THINGS YOU ARE GRATEFUL FOR.

_____
_____
_____
_____
_____

_____
_____
_____
_____

_____
_____
_____
_____
_____

HOW DOES GRATITUDE SHIFT MY PERSPECTIVE ON LIFE?

DAY 08
SETTING BOUNDARIES

> "I RESPECT MYSELF AND MY BOUNDARIES."

WHERE DO I NEED TO SET CLEARER BOUNDARIES?

Identify one area in your life where boundaries are needed.

HOW WILL SETTING THIS BOUNDARY IMPROVE MY WELL-BEING?

_____

_____

_____

_____

_____

_____

_____

_____

DAY 09

EXPLORING PASSIONS

> ## "I PURSUE WHAT SETS MY SOUL ON FIRE."

WHAT ACTIVITIES MAKE ME LOSE TRACK OF TIME?

LIST THREE PASSIONS YOU WOULD LIKE TO EXPLORE FURTHER.

HOW CAN I INCORPORATE THESE PASSIONS INTO MY DAILY ROUTINE?

DAY 10

BUILDING RESILIENCE

> "I AM RESILIENT AND CAN OVERCOME ANY CHALLENGE."

HOW HAVE I OVERCOME PAST CHALLENGES?

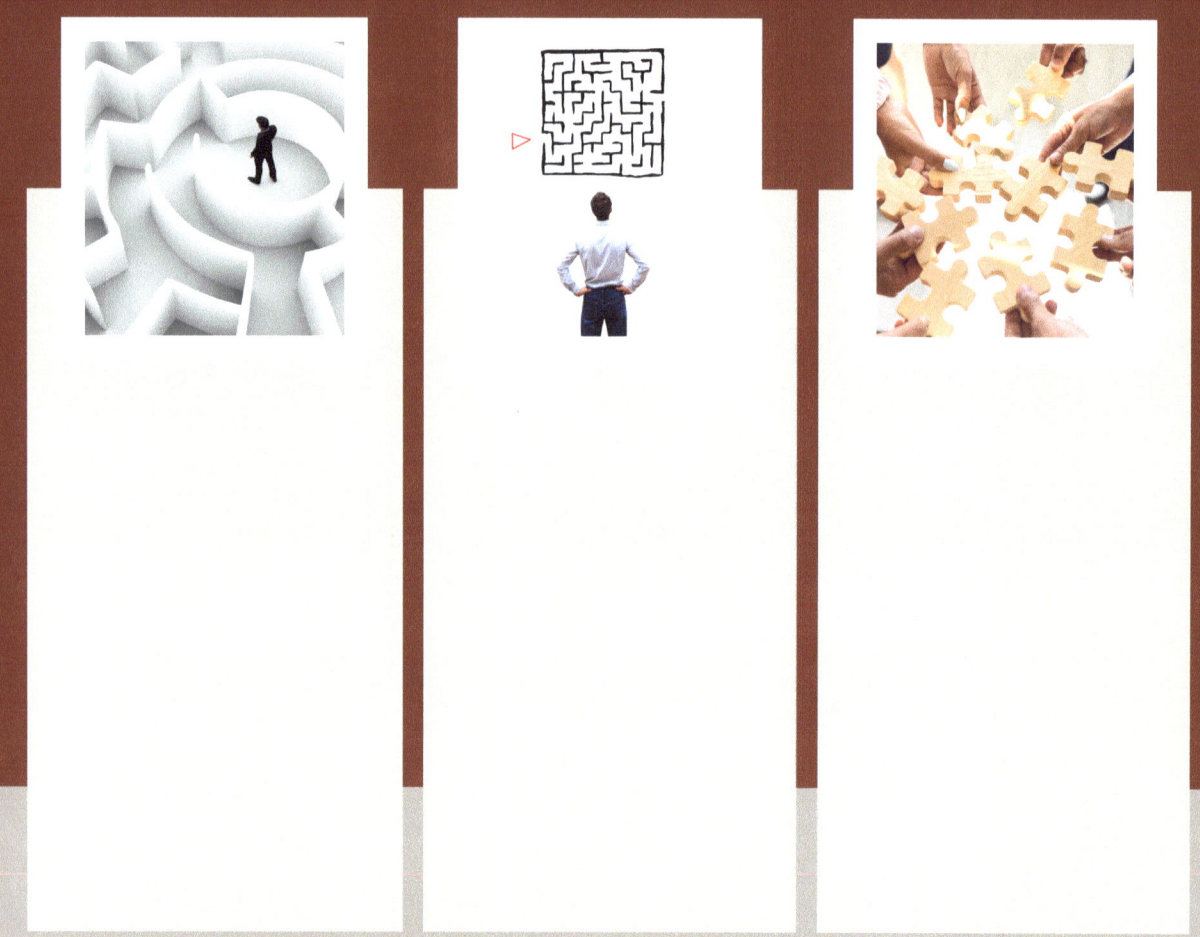

Write about a difficult situation you overcame and the lessons learned.

HOW CAN THESE LESSONS HELP ME FACE CURRENT CHALLENGES?

DAY 11
FOSTERING CREATIVITY

> "CREATIVITY FLOWS THROUGH ME EFFORTLESSLY."

WHEN DO I FEEL MOST CREATIVE?

DRAW OR WRITE SOMETHING THAT EXPRESSES HOW YOU FEEL NOW.

HOW DOES CREATIVITY ENHANCE MY PROBLEM-SOLVING SKILLS?

DAY 12
ENHANCING SELF-CARE

> **"TAKING CARE OF MYSELF IS A PRIORITY."**

PLAN A SELF-CARE DAY WITH ACTIVITIES YOU LOVE.

Day 1 **Day 2** **Day 3**

How does self-care impact my overall well-being?

WHAT SELF-CARE PRACTICES NOURISH ME?

DAY 13

DEVELOPING MINDFULNESS

> "I LIVE IN THE PRESENT MOMENT WITH EASE AND JOY."

SPEND FIVE MINUTES MEDITATING OR PRACTICING DEEP BREATHING.

What changes do I notice when I focus on the present moment?

DAY 14

BUILDING HEALTHY RELATIONSHIPS

> "I ATTRACT POSITIVE AND SUPPORTIVE RELATIONSHIPS."

WHO ARE THE PEOPLE THAT UPLIFT ME?

REACH OUT TO SOMEONE WHO INSPIRES YOU AND EXPRESS GRATITUDE.

Person 1

Person 2

Person 3

How can I nurture these positive relationships further?

DAY 15

EMBRACING FORGIVENESS

> "I FORGIVE MYSELF AND OTHERS FOR PAST MISTAKES."

WHO OR WHAT DO I NEED TO FORGIVE?

_____
_____
_____
_____
_____
_____
_____
_____
_____

WRITE A FORGIVENESS LETTER (YOU DON'T HAVE TO SEND IT).

DAY 16

HARNESSING INNER STRENGTH

> "MY INNER STRENGTH GUIDES ME THROUGH LIFE'S CHALLENGES."

WHAT ARE MY GREATEST STRENGTHS?

IDENTIFY THREE STRENGTHS AND THINK OF WAYS TO USE THEM MORE OFTEN.

Strength 1   **Strength 2**   **Strength 3**

How can these strengths help me achieve my goals?

DAY 17

PRACTICING PATIENCE

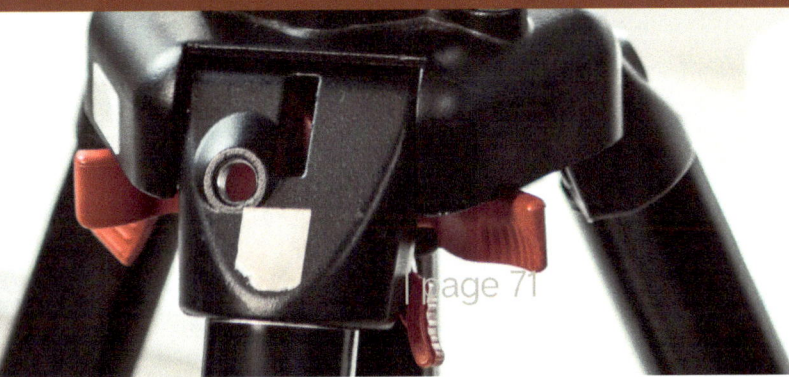

> "PATIENCE BRINGS CLARITY AND PEACE INTO MY LIFE."

IN WHAT AREAS OF LIFE DO I NEED MORE PATIENCE?

_____

_____

_____

_____

_____

_____

_____

_____

_____

PRACTICE PATIENCE TODAY BY SLOWING DOWN IN ONE TASK. HOW DID SLOWING DOWN MAKE YOU FEEL?

DAY 18
CULTIVATING JOY

"

"JOY FILLS EVERY MOMENT OF MY DAY."

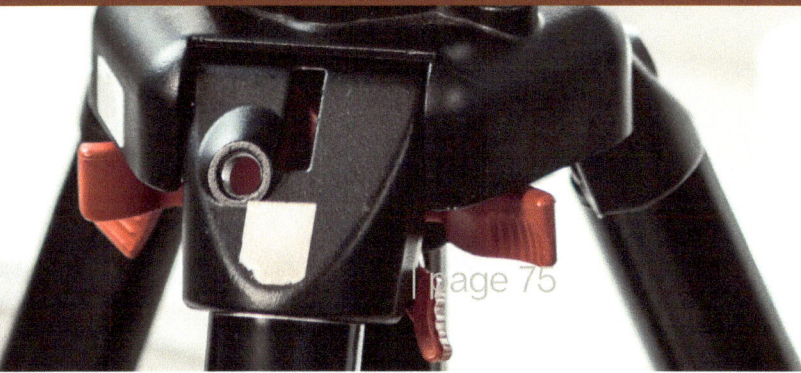

WHAT ACTIVITIES BRING ME JOY?

HOW CAN I BRING MORE JOY INTO EVERYDAY LIFE? WRITE THREE FUN THINGS TO DO.

Fun   **Fun**   **Fun**

How can I bring more joy into everyday life?

DAY 19

EMBRACING AUTHENTICITY

> "I AM TRUE TO MYSELF IN EVERY SITUATION."

REFLECT ON MOMENTS WHEN YOU WERE TRUE TO YOURSELF.

DAY 20

CREATING ACTION PLAN

> "I TAKE INSPIRED ACTION TOWARDS ACHIEVING DREAMS."

WHAT STEPS DO I NEED TO TAKE TO REACH MY GOALS?

Step 1   **Step 2**   **Step 3**

What support/resources do I need to succeed?

BREAK DOWN ONE GOAL IN ACTIONABLE STEPS.

DAY 21

REFLECTING ON YOUR JOURNEY AHEAD

> "GRATEFUL JOURNEY TRANSFORMATION UNDERGONE."

Vision Board Creation Tips

Goals

Create short-term goals (6 months - 12 months). Create long-term goals (1 - 3 years).

ADD AFFIRMATIONS AND QUOTES.

Be Specific

Write out 10 goals that you want to accomplish and select 1 - 3 and focus on them. Categories include health, fitness, career, money, vacation, education, and fun.

INCLUDE DATES AND DEADLINES FOR EACH GOAL.

Add Photos

Include photos of you, your friends and family to add a personal touch.

PHOTOS WILL BRING YOUR BOARD TO LIFE!

REFLECTION OF YOUR 21 DAY JOURNEY

_____
_____
_____
_____
_____
_____
_____
_____
_____
_____
_____
_____
_____
_____
_____
_____
_____

CREATE YOUR *Vision Board Below*

Vision Board Supply List

- Magazines
- Markers
- Stickers
- Index cards
- Bling stickers
- Affirmations
- Scissors
- Stick Glue

www.ingramcontent.com/pod-product-compliance
Lightning Source LLC
Chambersburg PA
CBHW041432010526
44118CB00002B/55